THE WASHINGTON *Monument*

MYTHS, Legends, and FACTS

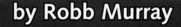

contributed ... in aid of the erect...
WASHINGTON NATIONAL
which entitles ...
privileges of Memb...
National M...

WASHINGTON
NATIONAL MONUMENT

by Robb Murray

Consultant:
Richard Bell
Associate Professor of History
University of Maryland
College Park, Maryland

CAPSTONE PRESS
a capstone imprint

Fact Finders Books are published by Capstone Press,
1710 Roe Crest Drive, North Mankato, Minnesota 56003
www.capstonepub.com

Library of Congress Cataloging-in-Publication Data
Cataloging-in-publication information is on file with the Library of Congress.
ISBN 978-1-4914-0206-1 (library binding)
ISBN 978-1-4914-0211-5 (pbk.)
ISBN 978-1-4914-0215-3 (ebook pdf)

Editorial Credits
Bobbie Nuytten, lead designer; Charmaine Whitman, production specialist

Developed and Produced by Focus Strategic Communications, Inc.
Adrianna Edwards: project manager
Ron Edwards, Kelly Stern: editors
Rob Scanlan: designer and compositor
Mary Rose MacLachlan: media researcher
Francine Geraci: copy editor and proofreader
Wendy Scavuzzo: fact checker

Photo Credits
Bridgeman Art Library: Barbara Loe Collection/Look and Learn, 9, Christie's Images/Private Collection, 12, Peter
Newark American Pictures/Private Collection, 8; Deborah Crowle Illustrations, 5; Library of Congress, cover (back),
1 (back), 6, 11, 13, 14, 22, 25, 27; National Park Service: Washington Monument, 17, 28, 29; North Wind Picture
Archives, 18; Shutterstock: Alan Kraft, 20, Ambient Ideas, cover (bottom), back cover, 1 (bottom), 3, artestudio8, 21,
Celso Diniz, cover (middle), 1 (middle), Daniel M. Silva, 24 (top), Hang Dinh, 23, justasc, 15, Orhan Cam, 24 (bottom),
Richard Thornton, 26, Steve Collender, 4; SuperStock, 16, Buyenlarge, 10, Stock Connection, 7

Design Elements by Shutterstock

Printed in the United States of America in Stevens Point, Wisconsin.
032014   008092WZF14

Table of Contents

MYSTERIOUS MONUMENT

The Washington Monument stands tall over the Reflecting Pool in the National Mall in Washington, D.C.

It stands tall, as tall as the legend of the man for whom it is named. It is the Washington Monument, the majestic **obelisk** that honors President George Washington. It is a landmark that towers over everything else in the nation's capital. The monument took decades to build and attracts millions of visitors each year. But there is more to this monument than meets the eye. Just as Washington has become the subject of myth and legends, so has his monument.

Some of the myths began with the man behind the monument. As the nation's first president and honored war hero, Washington was a man of myth and legends. He has been honored in statues, paintings, and on the dollar bill. But one monument stands above the rest.

obelisk: a four-sided stone pillar that tapers toward the top, which is shaped like a pyramid

The idea for a national monument to Washington dates back to 1783. Congress proposed that a statue of Washington be built to honor the first president. But plans for this statue stalled. It would take 65 years before the first stone in the current monument was placed.

Choosing a New Capital

When Washington became president in 1789, talks began about choosing a place for the nation's capital. Washington chose the present location of the District of Columbia on the Potomac River, between Maryland and Virginia. It would become the new capital in 1800.

Washington, D.C.

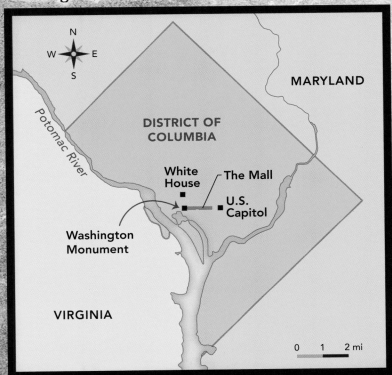

FACT

Not only the nation's capital is named after Washington. Across the country, dozens of cities, towns, and townships are named after the first president. There are also several bridges, schools, and neighborhoods, as well as the state of Washington, that remember him by using his name.

Planning the Capital District

Many people believed that the new country deserved a grand spectacle as part of its capital city. Washington hired an **engineer** named Pierre L'Enfant to draw up some plans.

L'Enfant's city design centered around the National Mall, stretching from the Potomac River to the Capitol Building. It also included places for a presidential residence, later named the White House, and a monument to Washington. The layout of these three important structures was intended to inspire the nation's leaders. The monument could be seen clearly from the Capitol and the White House.

engineer: a person who uses science and math to plan, design, or build

The city's design is mostly as L'Enfant envisioned.

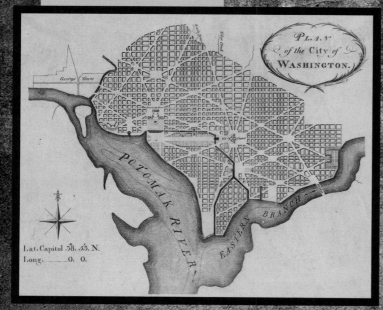

The President's Priorities

As president, Washington had to oversee both the development of the city and the building of the monument. But he decided that the nation's capital was more important than a statue to honor himself. Washington left office in 1797 and died two years later. Following his death, plans for a national monument to the nation's first president began to take shape again. But it was nearly 50 years before it really got under way.

the National Mall today

FACT

The Washington Monument, together with the Capitol and White House, were intended to form a perfect right triangle. It didn't work out that way, though. The land around the chosen location for the monument proved to be too soft and wet. So the monument was moved about 300 feet (91 meters) to where it stands today.

WHY WASHINGTON?

It was December 1776, and General George Washington and the Continental army were losing the American **Revolutionary War.** The better-equipped and larger British army had won several major battles. Washington's troops were low on supplies and weapons. Then Washington got an idea. He didn't have more men, he didn't have better weapons, and he didn't have more battle experience. But he did have the element of surprise.

At midnight December 26, Washington quietly led his troops across the icy Delaware River. From there, they ambushed the sleeping British soldiers. The Continental army won its first major victory of the war—the Battle of Trenton. The war would continue for nearly five more years until the British surrendered at Yorktown in 1781. Washington became a national hero. But his impact on the country did not start or end there.

Washington was the commander of the Continental army.

Revolutionary War (1775–1783): the American Colonies' fight for freedom from Great Britain; the Colonies later became the United States of America

GEORGE WASHINGTON AND THE CHERRY TREE

Many myths surround Washington. One of the most popular stories is Washington and the cherry tree. As a boy, Washington is said to have cut down a cherry tree. The myth says that when his father asked for the truth, George reportedly told him: "I cannot tell a lie. I chopped down the cherry tree." Experts believe the man who wrote the first book about Washington invented this story.

Many people still believe young George Washington chopped down a cherry tree.

A New Leader for a New Country

After Britain's defeat, Washington retired from public life. He was a role model and hero for many people. In 1787 Washington joined the Constitutional Convention and was elected its leader. That year the new U.S. Constitution was approved, and Washington was soon elected the nation's first president. People thought his actions on the battlefield made him a great choice. Washington actually served as president for two terms: from 1789 to 1797.

Washington is often referred to as the "Father of the Country."

WASHINGTON'S WOODEN TEETH

Another popular myth about Washington surrounds his wooden teeth. According to the story, Washington lost most of his teeth. He then had them replaced with a set of wooden ones. But this is only a myth. It is true that Washington had trouble with his teeth all his life. He lost one after another. But he did not wear wooden teeth. He wore **dentures** made of bone, hippopotamus ivory, human teeth, brass screws, lead, and gold metal wire.

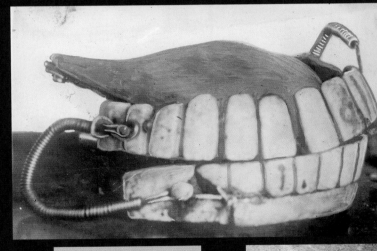

George Washington's false teeth

dentures: a set of false teeth

BUILDING THE MONUMENT

The Washington Monument saw many delays before the first stone was placed. The Washington National Monument Society was founded in 1833. Within four years the society had failed to raise enough money to begin construction on a monument. But the group had enough money to hold competitions for monument designs.

Several ideas were considered and then set aside. One of the first ideas was a statue of Washington on a horse. This **equestrian** figure was rejected because it was considered too small for a man of Washington's importance. Another proposal was for a statue in the shape of a pyramid. This pyramid was similar to the Great Seal of the United States on today's dollar bill. But that design was turned down as well.

Washington was known as an excellent horseback rider.

equestrian: having to do with horseback riding

The winning design finally came from Robert Mills, an architect from South Carolina. His original idea was to have a pillar with 30 100-foot (30-m) columns surrounding it. The design was eventually trimmed down to the single stone structure that stands today.

Robert Mills' original monument design

WASHINGTON NATIONAL MONUMENT

Getting Started

The Washington Monument was built in two bursts of construction. The first was between 1848 and 1854 and the second between 1877 and 1884. The first phase is often referred to as the "private" phase of development. Money for this construction phase was raised by private individuals, not the government.

Construction finally began, and on July 4, 1848, a crowd of about 20,000 people attended a ceremony to lay the monument's cornerstone. The cornerstone was laid on the bed of the foundation. It was buried below the ground.

President James K. Polk presided, and many prominent Washington politicians attended. Three future U.S. presidents, James Buchanan, Abraham Lincoln, and Andrew Johnson, were present.

ceremony to lay the Washington Monument's cornerstone

CORNERSTONE

The cornerstone was solid marble and weighed 24,500 pounds (11,100 kilograms). Several historical objects were buried in the cornerstone. These included copies of the U.S. Constitution and Declaration of Independence, plans for the monument, books, reports, atlases, and maps, as well as a portrait of Washington.

A copy of the U.S. Constitution is one of the objects buried in the Washington Monument cornerstone.

Construction Delays

After the cornerstone was placed, up went the monument, stone by stone. Within a few years, it had reached a height of more than 150 feet (45 m). Then, a lack of money halted the project. Getting the monument to that height had cost $300,000. The group overseeing the monument's construction was forced to wait. More money had to be was raised.

From 1854 to 1876, the monument sat unfinished and abandoned. Famous American writer Mark Twain called the incomplete structure "an eyesore." During the Civil War (1861–1865), the grounds around the half-finished monument became a cattle yard for the Union army. No construction took place during the war years.

Construction of the Washington Monument stopped in 1854 after six years of work.

DONATED STONES

The Washington National Monument Society asked different groups to donate stones for the monument's construction. Many stones arrived from all over the United States and from around the world. Some had the names of states, and some had the names of individual cities. Others were from different branches of the military.

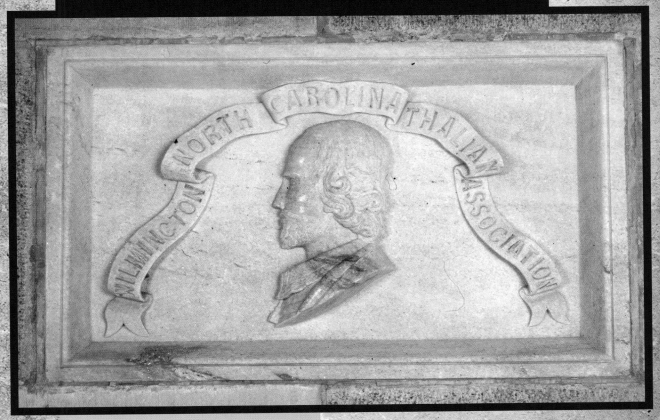

North Carolina was one of many states that donated stones for the monument.

Finishing the Monument

Finally, work on the monument resumed in 1876. Congress appointed Lieutenant Colonel Thomas Lincoln Casey of the U.S. Corps of Engineers to oversee the completion of the project. That year was the 100th anniversary of the signing of the Declaration of Independence. Congress used that occasion to approve funds to complete the monument.

The second phase of construction proceeded quickly. At about the 470-foot (143-m) level, builders began angling the walls inward. This angle would strengthen the walls so they could support the 3,300-pound (1,497-kg) **capstone**.

The finishing touch was an aluminum pyramid put in place in December 1884. At the time, aluminum was a very rare metal. After 36 years, the monument was finally finished.

capstone: the final stone that completes a building or other structure

The aluminum cap was designed to act as a lightning rod. It still works today.

Washington Monument: Construction Timeline

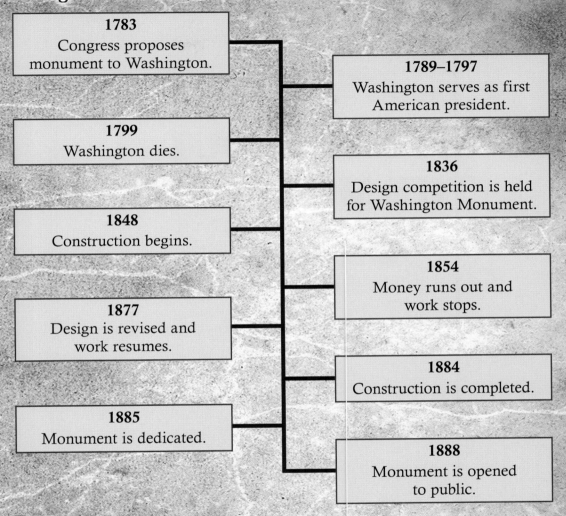

1783
Congress proposes monument to Washington.

1789–1797
Washington serves as first American president.

1799
Washington dies.

1836
Design competition is held for Washington Monument.

1848
Construction begins.

1854
Money runs out and work stops.

1877
Design is revised and work resumes.

1884
Construction is completed.

1885
Monument is dedicated.

1888
Monument is opened to public.

FACT When completed the Washington Monument was the world's tallest structure at 555 feet (169 m) high. A few years later, it was surpassed by the Eiffel Tower in Paris. The tower stands 1,063 feet (324 m) high. The monument, however, remains the world's tallest all-stone structure and the world's tallest obelisk.

MYTHS ABOUT THE MONUMENT

Curious Coloring

Even before the Washington Monument was completed, myths and legends about it began to grow. People gazing at the Washington Monument often notice it has two shades of gray. About a third of the way up the column, there is a ring of contrasting stone. Some people believe a flood caused the ring. But the line on the monument is the result of the delays in construction. So many years passed between the time construction stopped and then restarted that stones from a different location had to be used. The two **quarries** produced stones of two different colors.

contrasting stone colors of the Washington Monument

quarry: a place where stone or other minerals are dug from the ground

QUARRIES

The stone in a quarry is removed from the ground by cutting and blasting. First, the dirt is cleared away from the stone. Then drills bore into the rock, and dynamite is used to blast the rock free. Slices of stone are cut away layer by layer. A block of marble can weigh up to 25,000 pounds (11,000 kg). These enormous chunks are cut up into smaller sizes and removed from the quarry.

a block of cut stone being removed at a quarry

21

Hidden Messages

The aluminum cap on the top of the Washington Monument contains a hidden message. A myth surrounds the writing on the monument's cap. The top of the monument has messages no one sees, including one written in Latin. It says "Laus Deo," which means "Praise be to God." The other sides of the aluminum cap have inscriptions too. One side says, "Cornerstone laid on bed of foundation July 4, 1848." The other two sides list the names of the men who helped build it.

cap of the Washington Monument with inscription

Tall Tale

There are also myths about the height of the monument. One story says that no building in Washington, D.C., can be taller than the Washington Monument. Not so. The law states that no building can be taller than 130 feet (40 m).

The Washington Monument is about 550 feet (168 m) high, but it was built before the law was passed. Even so, it is not the tallest structure in the city. The National **Cathedral** is actually taller. The building is only about 300 feet (91 m) from the ground up. But since the cathedral sits on a hill, it is 676 feet (206 m) above sea level. That is nearly 100 feet (30 m) higher than the Washington Monument.

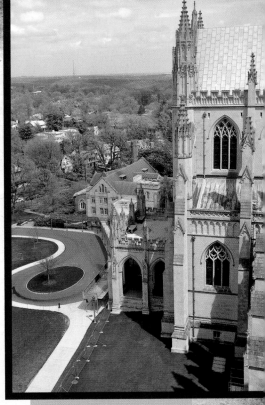

Cathedral Church of Saint Peter and Saint Paul is the official name of the Washington National Cathedral.

cathedral: a large, important church

MONUMENT STATISTICS

- 555 feet, 5⅛ inches (169.3 m) tall
- weighs 90,854 tons (82,421 metric tons)
- 36,491 individual stones of marble and granite
- 897 steps from bottom to top (with 50 landings)
- column width at base: 55 feet, 1 inch (16.8 m)
- column width at top: 34 feet, 5½ inches (10.5 m)
- wall thickness at base: 15 feet (4.57 m)
- wall thickness at top: 18 inches (0.457 m)

Resting Place

Another popular myth is that Washington is actually buried under the monument named for him. But he is not. Washington is buried at his Virginia estate, Mount Vernon, in a tomb with his wife, Martha.

Washington's tomb at Mount Vernon

Washington and his wife, Martha, lived at Mount Vernon for 40 years.

Stolen Stone

As construction progressed in the mid-1800s, different groups contributed memorial stones for the monument. But not all of these stones got used. Pope Pius IX, the head of the Roman Catholic Church, sent a stone for the monument. The marble stone had been part of a famous church in Rome called the Temple of Concord.

Members of the Know-Nothing Party are believed to have stolen this stone. Members of this group distrusted many political and religious groups, including Catholics. It is believed that members of this group broke into the monument construction site and stole the pope's stone. According to the myth, they dumped the stone in the Potomac River. The stone has never been found.

FROM THE
JEFFERSON SOCIETY OF THE
UNIVERSITY OF VIRGINIA
TO THE NATIONAL WASHINGTON
MONUMENT
JANUARY 7TH 1860

Nearly 200 memorial stones are mounted inside the monument. The stones were donated by groups and individuals around the world.

THE MONUMENT TODAY

Ever since the Washington Monument first opened, it has been a popular destination for visitors to the nation's capital. The first year it opened, it was reported that more than 120,000 people visited the site. Today about 500,000 people visit the Washington Monument each year.

visitors at the Washington Monument

Renovations

Although the monument was completed in 1888, work continues on it today. Wind, rain, and snow wear the stones and mortar away. The monument has been renovated or restored four times in the 130 years since it was completed.

The first restoration took place in 1934, one year after the National Parks Service took over managing the monument. Thirty years later, a second maintenance project was completed. Then in 1998, the monument underwent a massive restoration project to clean and repair all the stone surfaces.

Scaffolding covered the Washington Monument during the 1998 restoration.

27

Earthquake

The fourth restoration took place following an earthquake in 2011. On August 22 a massive earthquake rocked the eastern United States. It was centered in Virginia and caused much damage in Washington, D.C.

At the time of the quake, people were inside the Washington Monument's observation deck. No one was seriously injured. Everyone got out safely. But several pieces of stone came loose, and officials found a large **fissure** in the top of the monument. The crack was 1 inch (2.5 centimeters) wide and 4 feet (1.2 m) long. The monument was then closed to the public.

During the following few months, two expert teams scaled the outside of the monument using mountain climbing gear. They patched the monument in several places, but major repairs were required. Repairs to the monument cost about $15 million.

earthquake damage to the Washington Monument

fissure: a split or crack especially in rock or stone

Keeping the Washington Monument in good condition is an ongoing project. With every repair or restoration comes new myths surrounding this amazing monument to Washington. But battling the wind and water damage ensures that the Washington Monument continues to stand tall for people to visit and explore its mysteries.

FACT After the earthquake, a TV news report announced that there were concerns the monument may be tilting. The monument was inspected carefully, and no tilting was found.

Workers climb the Washington Monument after the 2011 earthquake.

GLOSSARY

capstone (KAP-stohn)—the final stone that completes a building or other structure

cathedral (kuh-THEE-druhl)—a large, important church

dentures (DEN-churz)—a set of false teeth

engineer (en-juh-NEER)—a person who uses science and math to plan, design, or build

equestrian (i-KWES-tree-uhn)—having to do with horseback riding

fissure (FISH-er)—a split or crack especially in rock or stone

obelisk (OB-uh-lisk)—a four-sided stone pillar that tapers toward the top, which is shaped like a pyramid

quarry (KWOR-ee)—a place where stone or other minerals are dug from the ground

Revolutionary War (1775–1783) (rev-uh-LOO-shun-air-ee WAR)—the American Colonies' fight for freedom from Great Britain; the Colonies later became the United States of America

READ MORE

Biskup, Agnieszka. *George Washington: The Rise of America's First President*. American Graphics. North Mankato, Minn.: Capstone Press, 2013.

Carr, Aaron. *Washington Monument*. American Icons. New York: AV2 by Weigl, 2014.

Nelson, Kristin L. *The Washington Monument*. Famous Places. Minneapolis: Lerner Publishing, 2011.

Ransom, Candice F. *George Washington and the Story of the U.S. Constitution*. Minneapolis: Lerner Classroom, 2011.

CRITICAL THINKING USING THE COMMON CORE

1. Reread the section, A New Leader for a New Country (p. 10). What is the main idea in this section? What details support this main idea? How did you decide the main idea? (Key Ideas and Details)

2. Reread the section, Finishing the Monument (pp. 18). How is this section organized? What text features helped you decide the organization? What evidence was the most useful for your decision? Why? (Craft and Structure)

3. Reread these sections, Renovations (p. 27) and Earthquake (pp. 28–29). What point is the author making in this section? What evidence is provided to prove this point? Why do you think the author wrote about this? (Integration of Knowledge and Ideas)

INTERNET SITES

FactHound offers a safe, fun way to find Internet sites related to this book. All of the sites on FactHound have been researched by our staff.

Here's all you do:

Visit www.facthound.com

Type in this code: 9781491402061

Check out projects, games, and lots more at
www.capstonekids.com

INDEX